DON E. BEYER

THE TOTEM POLE INDIANS OF THE NORTHWEST

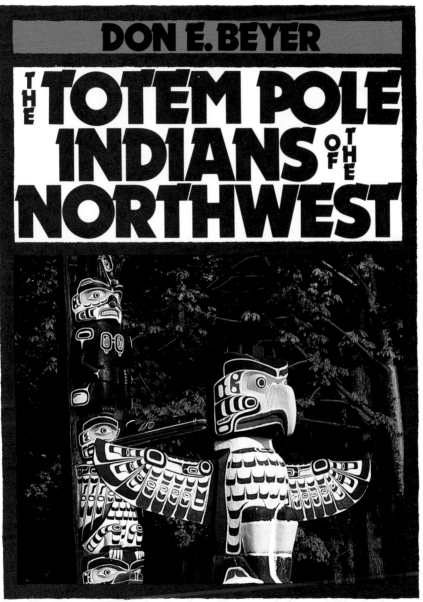

Franklin Watts   New York   London   Toronto   Sydney   A First Book   1989

First Paperback Edition 1991

Library of Congress Cataloging-in-Publication Data

Beyer, Don E.
The totem pole Indians of the Northwest / by Don E. Beyer.
p.   cm.—(A First book)
Includes index.
Summary: Describes the lifestyle and culture of the totem pole
Indians of the Pacific Northwest.
ISBN 0-531-10750-7 (lib.)/ISBN 0-531-15607-9 (pbk.)
1. Indians of North America—Northwest Coast of North America—
Juvenile literature. [1. Indians of North America—Northwest
Coast of North America—Social life and customs.]   I. Title.
II. Series.
E78.N78B48   1989
979.5'00497—dc19   89-31170   CIP   AC

CONTENTS

*Thank you to all who helped
in the writing of this book*

*particularly my wife,
Georgette Frazer*

*my longtime friend,
Alden Carter*

*and my friend and
colleague, Edward Arendt*

*For my terrific sons,
Hawthorne and Trevelyan*

THE LAND AND THE PEOPLE

Five hundred years ago, on the north coast of Washington state near Ozette, a Makah Indian village stretched along the Pacific Ocean for nearly a mile. It was a night in June. Heavy rains had fallen for many days and had soaked the steep hillside behind the village of big, cedarwood houses.

Inside, family groups slept on raised platforms around a central fire. Wrapped in animal skins, they lay on mats woven of reeds and bark. Around them, baskets and wooden boxes held clothing, tools, fishing and hunting gear, and the other items of daily life. One house contained a special totem carving, which looked like the back fin of a killer whale. The wood carving was painted black and decorated with hundreds of otter teeth. Under another house nearby, a litter of puppies snuggled in the warmth of their mother.

Suddenly the steep hillside behind the houses collapsed. Thousands of tons of rain-loosened blue mud slid over part of the village and smothered everything in its path—houses, people, dogs—in a wet and muddy grave.

The mudslide that destroyed part of the village also preserved its remains. In 1970, a heavy storm washed away some of the mud and uncovered the wood of houses that had been buried for five hundred years. Archaeologists (scholars who uncover and study the remains of the past) were called in to investigate. They began a dig that lasted eleven years. Thousands of artifacts (man-made objects) were found. These included household furnishings and tools, canoe paddles, fishing hooks, pieces of clothing, weaving looms, whaling harpoons, wood carvings, and many other objects that help us to understand how the Makah people lived centuries ago.

The Makah were one of a number of Indian groups who lived along the Pacific coast from Washington state to Alaska. Together these tribes are called the people of the totem pole after the largest of the famous wood carvings that were made by some of the tribes. We have come to know them from archaeological studies, from the writings of early explorers, and

ARCHAEOLOGY STUDENTS
AT THE SITE OF THE MAKAH
INDIAN VILLAGE THAT WAS
BURIED IN A MUD SLIDE
FIVE HUNDRED YEARS AGO.

THE STUDENTS SPRAY AWAY
MUD BENEATH WHICH THEY
HAVE FOUND SUCH OBJECTS
AS THIS OWL'S HEAD.

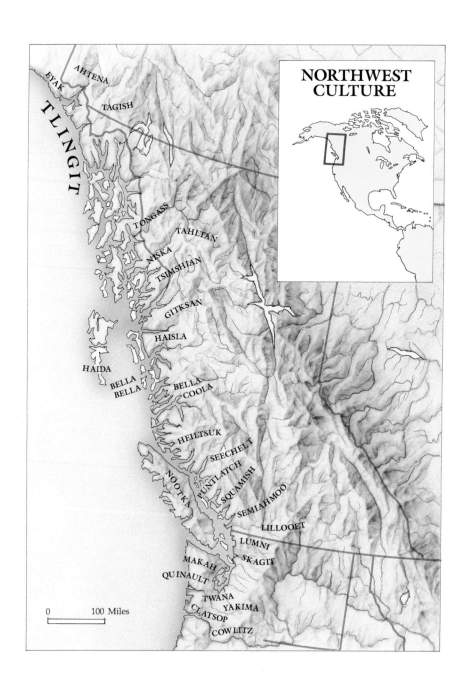

NORTHWEST
CULTURE

TLINGIT

EYAK

AHTENA

TAGISH

TONGASS

TAHLTAN

NISKA

TSIMSHIAN

GITKSAN

HAISLA

HAIDA

BELLA
BELLA

BELLA
COOLA

HEILTSUK

SEECHELT

PUNTLATCH

SQUAMISH

NOOTKA

SEMIAHMOO

LILLOOET

LUMNI

SKAGIT

MAKAH

QUINAULT

TWANA

YAKIMA

CLATSOP

COWLITZ

0   100 Miles

from the study of Indian groups living today. Like their homeland, the life of these people was rich and colorful.

The land of the totem pole makers is a world of snow-capped mountains, broad blue ocean, rushing rivers, and wet green forests. It is a long, narrow slice of coast about a thousand miles (1,600 km) from north to south and not much more than a hundred miles (160 km) wide.

Totem pole land begins in Washington state. It extends north into Canada, covering the coast and islands of British Columbia, and ends at the Alaskan panhandle around Yakutat Bay. This rugged place of islands, peninsulas, and bays is sandwiched between the Pacific Ocean to the west and a long wall of mountains in the east.

The mountains and the ocean combine to create a moderate climate that is cool in the summer and quite warm (rarely below freezing) in the winter for being so far north. The warm waters of the Japan Current move along the coast to keep the temperature up. Winds blowing in from the ocean are loaded with moisture that drops as rain when clouds reach the coastal mountains. This happens often, and rainfall of 160 inches (406 cm) or more a year is common. The rain and mild temperature encourage the growth of great stands of redwood, cedar, and fir trees. Dark and wet, the forests are often carpeted in green moss that runs up the trunks of trees. Forest lands are home to a wide variety of plants and many animals.

The ancestors of the totem pole people came into this area from the north as early as ten thousand years ago. They found a land with a mild climate where food was plentiful and easily obtained from the ocean and forest. The materials needed for clothing and shelter were all around. The Indians settled inland by large rivers, at river mouths where the rushing water ran into the sea, in pockets of flat land between the sea and mountains, and on the many forest-covered islands of the coastal waters.

Because of the rugged land, groups were often cut off from one another. This is why they came to speak different languages and have ways of life that were a bit different from one place to another.

Seven main groups of people lived in the land of the totem pole. In the south, the Coast Salish (Saylish) settled in northern Washington State around Puget Sound and in lower British Columbia. The Nootka (Noot-ka) or Nuchanulth, who were great whale hunters and canoe makers, centered on Vancouver Island. They may have been the first of the coast people to have contact with European explorers and to trade with them. Further north, on the coast of British Co-

A NOOTKA MAN. THE NOOTKA WERE ONE OF THE SEVEN MAIN GROUPS OF PEOPLE LIVING IN THE PACIFIC NORTHWEST.

lumbia, lived the Kwakiutl (Kwag-key-yooth) and their close neighbors, the Bella Coola (Bell-a Cool-a). The Queen Charlotte Islands of British Columbia were the ancient home of the Haida (Hi-duh), who were known as great sailors and fierce soldiers in war. The northern coast of British Columbia, in the area of the port city of Prince Rupert, was settled by the Tsimshian (Tsim-shan). And in the far north of totem pole land lived the Tlingit (Kling-git), whose settlement area extended from northern British Columbia to the panhandle of Alaska and included all the islands in between.

It is estimated that by the year 1800 there may have been one hundred thousand people living in the totem pole lands of the northwest coast. More Indian people lived closer together there than anywhere else in North America.

HUNTING AND GATHERING FOOD

The Indians of the Northwest were hunters and gatherers. They grew very little food. The ocean and the forests supplied more than enough for their needs.

Fishing was the most important way of getting food. To the tribes on the other side of the mountains, the coastal people were known as "the Fish Eaters."

Fish were caught with nets, rakes, traps, spears, harpoons, and hooks. The hooks were made of wood, bone, or shell. Some hooks were made large to catch big fish such as the halibut, which weighed as much as 500 pounds (227 kg).

In the early spring the Nootka went to sea in canoes and used rakelike tools to gather herring, which

THE NORTHWEST INDIANS WERE VERY
DEPENDENT UPON FISHING.

THOUSANDS OF CANDLEFISH DRY ON
RACKS. CANDLEFISH WERE A SOURCE OF
ARTIFICIAL LIGHT FOR THE INDIANS.

moved along the coast in large schools. Rakes were also used to catch fish called olachen or candlefish. These little fish were so oily that a dried olachen with a wick run through it could be used as a candle. Olachen oil was also widely used in the cooking and preserving of other food.

Dogfish, smelt, cod, flounder, and sturgeon were other fish taken from the sea, but the salmon were the main catch. In many languages spoken on the coast, the word for fish and salmon was the same.

Salmon were easiest to catch in the fall when they swam from the ocean into the rivers to lay and fertilize their eggs. Fishermen made fences of tree saplings to channel the fish toward waiting nets as the salmon swam upstream. The Indians pulled the big salmon from the water by the thousands.

This was one of the busiest times of the year. Men, women, and children worked to dry and smoke the salmon over slow fires. This provided the main food supply for the winter months. Because the salmon were so important to Indian life, they were the subject of many stories and legends.

Indians believed that salmon were people in the form of fish who left a magic village under the ocean to provide food for others. In appreciation for this gift, the totem pole people performed a religious ceremony each year. The first fish of the season was roasted while prayers of thanks were said. Then the skeleton, believed to contain the fish spirit, was carefully placed in the river to return home and grow a new covering of flesh. By honoring the fish spirit in this way, Indians ensured the return of the salmon the next year.

The ocean provided other kinds of food. Shellfish, such as oysters, mussels, clams, and abalone, were eaten and their shells were used for tools and decorations. Sea mammals, including seals, sea lions, porpoises, sea otters, and whales, were important sources of food for some tribes.

The great whale hunters of the north coast were the Nootkas of British Columbia and their near relatives, the Makah. Whaling was a very dangerous activity. The men of wealthy families owned the boats and other equipment that were needed to hunt whales.

The twenty-foot (6 m) harpoons used to spear the whales were very heavy to throw a long distance. The whaleboat had to sneak up close to the animal to allow the hunter to drive the harpoon into its side. Getting that near to a huge whale was risky. When the whale felt the barbed point of the harpoon, it dove deep with violent slaps of its huge tail. The boatmen had to paddle fast and hard to get away without being crushed by the whale.

Attached to the harpoon was a rope with floats. These air bags of sealskin worked like brakes to slow

DRYING SALMON IN A VILLAGE ALONG THE COLUMBIA RIVER. DUE TO A MILD CLIMATE, THE INDIANS WERE ABLE TO CATCH ENOUGH SALMON DURING SPAWNING SEASON TO LAST THE REST OF THE YEAR.

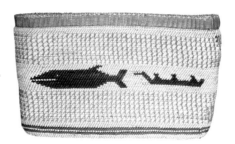

WHALING WAS IMPORTANT TO THE NORTHWEST INDIANS' WAY OF LIFE, AND THE WHALE WAS PROMINENT IN MANY OF THE PEOPLE'S CRAFTS. HERE A WOVEN BASKET DISPLAYS A WHALE AND CANOE DESIGN.

the whale's movement and to tire it out. The whale-boat followed closely and attacked the whale each time it came to the surface.

Not all foods came from the ocean. The forests supplied some variety to the diet of the coast Indians. At certain times of the year, the Indians picked wild strawberries, blackberries, and raspberries. The ripe berries were eaten fresh, made into fruit juice, or preserved in fish oil for the winter. Lettuce, onions, moss, and the root of the camas were other wild plants used as food in some places.

Certain parts of the Northwest coast offered good hunting of deer, bear, mountain sheep, and elk. Indians hunted ducks and geese when these birds migrated north and south.

Food was plentiful on the Northwest coast. There were some very busy times of food gathering and production. Other times were not so busy and people could do other things. This is why arts and crafts were so well developed in the land of the totem. People had lots of time to work on them.

ARTS AND CRAFTS

The Indians of the Pacific Northwest were excellent craftspersons and artists. When they needed things for their daily activities—baskets, boxes, blankets, cradles, clothing, canoes—they made them from materials nearby.

Of all of the arts and crafts the Indians practiced, the greatest was working with wood. Trees were as important to the life of the Indian as were fish. Many different kinds of trees grew in the wet, green forests along the ocean. Each had its special use.

The springy wood of the yew tree was excellent for making bows and harpoons. Soft yellow cedar and alder were easily carved into bowls, dishes, and spoons. The giant redwoods of the south coast were used for

THE PACIFIC NORTHWEST INDIANS WERE EXCEPTIONAL
CRAFTSPEOPLE, PARTICULARLY WHEN USING WOOD.
THE RATTLE (TOP) IS IN THE SHAPE OF A RAVEN, ONE
OF THE CHIEF FIGURES OF NORTHWEST COAST
MYTHOLOGY. CHESTS (MIDDLE) WERE SO TIGHTLY
CONSTRUCTED THEY WERE USED TO STORE FISH OIL.
THE TOTEM POLE (LEFT) WAS THE MOST SPECTACULAR
ACHIEVEMENT OF THE NORTHWEST ARTISTS. THIS ONE
FEATURES A RAVEN AT THE TOP AND OTHER FIGURES
IMPORTANT IN A CLAN'S MYTHOLOGICAL HISTORY.

building and canoe making. But the most widely available and useful tree was the red cedar.

The red cedar is a large evergreen tree. It can grow to 150 feet (46 m) tall and 8 feet (2.5 m) around. The wood is soft and easily worked. This was important because the Indians had few metal tools. The grain of the wood is straight and can be split into thick boards with a stone hammer and wedge. Indians used the red cedar to make houses, totem poles, boxes, masks, and many other smaller items.

Totem poles have become famous all over the world. Many people believe that all Indians in North America made such poles. This is not true. The original home of the totem pole is the Northwest coast.

The totem pole was a kind of sign. Today, signs in front of homes and businesses tell us about the people living and working inside. Signs often have both pictures and writing. Totem poles were something like that, though they looked very different from most signs today and had no writing on them.

A totem pole, which could be as tall as 80 feet (24 m), consisted of a group of carved figures called crests that perched on top of one another. These might be in the form of humans (family members), animals (bear, raven, wolf), or other creatures (thunderbird, sea serpent). Totem poles, with their beautifully carved and painted crests, had special meaning for the individual, the family, and the clan.

The house pole was a form of family history and an advertisement for important people. Its crests often told something about how the family began long ago. The house pole also identified the clan to which the family belonged. Sometimes it served as a reminder of an important event, such as a great battle, in which family members took part. Chiefs and other important people erected totem poles to let others know who they were. This was a way to establish their importance and power within the village and tribe. Only the richest people could afford the expense of having a pole carved.

The grave pole was made to honor the dead in the way that gravestones do today. Often a new chief would erect such a pole to honor the old chief who had recently died. Sometimes these poles held a box containing the body or ashes of the dead chief.

Carved poles had other uses as well. They might be placed near a beach to welcome visitors or to mark an owner's waterfront area. To anyone approaching the village by water, the forest of tall and painted poles along the beach and in front of the Big-Houses must have been an impressive sight.

The Indians chose trees for totem poles with great care. Often the best trees could only be found far from the village. Once it was cut down, the tree was stripped of its branches and bark. If it were very large, the tree might be hollowed out on one side. This not only made it lighter to move but also kept it from splitting. Men then floated the log to the village and dragged it to the place where the wood-carver began his work.

A good carver was an important man. He was paid well for his work and was honored among his people. Sometimes he was called to travel long distances to do work in other villages. He could be away a long time. Some poles took a year or more to complete.

The carver's training began in childhood. Having the skill to use the carving tools of stone, shell, and copper was only a part of his work. He was also in charge of painting the pole. The carver made paints by mixing minerals and animal materials with fish oil or salmon eggs. The villagers also expected the carver to have contact with spirits and to use spirit power in medicine songs and dances to make a good carving.

The carving of a totem pole was a big event in the life of a village. Among the Tsimshian and Tlingit people, a committee of clan elders and the local medicine man or woman supervised the carving to make sure that everything was done right. When the pole was finally set up, ceremonies and feasts called potlatches honored the event.

CARVED WOODEN MASKS COULD RESEMBLE BEASTS OR HUMANS. BY PULLING ON THE STRINGS OF THIS OCTOPUS MASK, THE TENTACLES MOVED AND THE MOUTH OPENED AND SHUT.

Carved wooden masks of cedar and other wood were a feature of many ceremonies on the Northwest coast. Like the crests on totem poles, they were made to represent humans, animals, and other creatures. Masks were beautifully carved and colorful. Mask makers used shells, teeth, bone, fur, feathers, hair, copper, and many other materials for decoration. Some masks were very large and had parts that moved.

The people of the totem pole used the largest red cedar trees to make boats and seagoing canoes. The largest canoes measured 60 feet (18 m) or more in length.

Cutting down a big tree to make a canoe was a very difficult job to do with simple tools. Usually the Indians built a fire at the base of the tree. They burned and scraped until, after much hard work, the great cedar came crashing to the ground.

The Indians then split the trunk in half the long way using stone hammers and wedges. Next the carvers hollowed out the inside to the proper thickness with fire and stone tools called adzes. After shaping the outside to run smoothly through the water, the Indians widened the inside by softening the wood with water and hot rocks. They then stretched the wood crossways with boards called thwarts. The very ends of the canoe were usually carved separately and attached with pegs and cords to make a watertight fit.

The Haida and Nootka were especially good canoe makers and boatmen. Their big canoes were paddled hundreds of miles in the dangerous waters along the coast.

THE PROW OF THIS HAIDA
CANOE DEPICTS A STYLIZED
WOLF. HAIDA CANOES OFTEN
MEASURED FIFTY FEET IN
LENGTH AND COULD CARRY
ABOUT SIXTY WARRIORS. THE
ELABORATE ORNAMENTS WERE
USUALLY FAMILY CRESTS.

The people of the totem also used the red cedar to construct houses. The Big-Houses, as they were called, were from 20 to 60 feet (6–18 m) wide and from 50 to 150 feet (15–46 m) long. The richest and most important families had the largest houses.

House building began with a frame of posts and logs. Workers notched these pieces on the ends and fastened them together with wooden pegs. They made walls of thick boards tied to the frame with cedar bark rope or roots. Overlapping cedar boards or large pieces of bark weighted down with stones covered the roof.

Inside and out, the Big-House was often decorated with painting and carving. The Haida people liked to paint the outside walls white and then make them beautiful with large designs and totem crests. Some groups used a totem pole with a hole through it as an entrance to the house.

Other crafts besides woodworking were important to the daily life of the village. The coastal people used many baskets for storage and carrying. They wove them of river reeds and grass. Very tightly made baskets held water for cooking. Animal designs or geometric patterns decorated much of the basket makers' work.

Women did most of the weaving of blankets and cloth. This was done on wooden frames called looms. Weavers used cedar bark for yarn and often mixed it

BASKETS SUCH AS THESE WERE USED
FOR STORAGE AND BERRY-PICKING.
BASKET WEAVING WAS USUALLY
DONE WHEN IT WAS RAINING
BECAUSE THE MATERIALS DRIED
OUT AT OTHER TIMES.

with mountain goat wool or dog hair. They decorated their work freely with geometric designs and painted totem crests.

Plants from marsh areas along the coast supplied the material for mats. Mats were made from reeds and cedar bark. The Indians used them for sitting and sleeping.

A WOVEN BLANKET WITH
A BROWN BEAR DESIGN

THE WORLD OF HUMANS AND SPIRITS

The Indians of the Northwest coast lived close to nature. The world of sky, mountain, forest, and ocean was their home. They believed that they shared this home with many spirits.

The Indians said that all things had spirits, including sun, moon, river, tree, mountain, human being, and animal. Spirits could take many forms. They could be without bodies, unseen and powerful. They could also take human form. Like humans, spirits had their own families, clans, and villages. When spirits traveled away from their kingdoms, they often took on animal bodies and became a salmon, bear, killer whale, wolf, or other creature. The Indians believed that the spirits of nature ran the world. If people respected and honored the spirits, their own lives would run smoothly. If they treated the spirits of nature badly, there might be serious trouble.

Many legends expressed Indian beliefs about the spirit powers that roamed the world. The legends were not written down, because the Indians had no writing. They were spoken stories told by many generations of parents to their children. For the people of the Northwest coast, the stories helped to explain how the world and the creatures in it came to be the way they were.

Many legends were widely known from north to south in the country of the totem pole makers. Others were local stories told by individual families or households. Some legends told how ancestors came to have the family name and use the totem crests of animal spirits.

For example, the people of the bear totem believed that their ancestors had been helped by the bear spirit long ago. As a result, they were given the right to use the bear name. Many of the Bear People believed that this totem gave them special power or skill to hunt and kill bears. Bear People wore bear pictures on their clothing and used bear masks in their ceremonies.

The Indians of the totem believed that some of their people had special control of spiritual and mag-

A SPIRIT FIGURE

THE SHAMANS USED VARIOUS TOOLS IN THEIR TRADE.

THE SHAMAN MASK AT LEFT DEPICTS AN EAGLE SPIRIT. WHEN A SHAMAN PUT ON A MASK, SHE OR HE WAS TRANSFORMED INTO THE SPIRIT SHOWN ON THE MASK. A SHAMAN'S WOODEN RATTLE (BELOW) DEPICTS AN OYSTER-CATCHER BIRD ON WHOSE BACK SIT THREE SMALL WITCHES BEING CARRIED THROUGH THE AIR BY A MOUNTAIN GOAT. WITCHES WERE MUCH FEARED BY THESE PEOPLE.

ical powers. These were men and women known as shamans. Shamans could contact spirits and use their power to make strong "medicine." People asked the shaman for help in preparing for hunting, war, or funerals.

In times of serious illness, people went to the shaman for a cure as they might go to a doctor today. Shamans knew how to use healing herbs and plants. People believed that shamans had special powers to cure illnesses that were caused by angry spirits and sorcery.

The power of shamans made people afraid. They went to a shaman only when they had a serious need. Otherwise, they believed it was better to stay away. When a shaman died, he or she was usually buried away from the other people of the village.

LIFE IN THE VILLAGE

Among the people of the totem, the family, the household, and the clan were the most important groups. It was through the family that children received their names, family history, certain rights and privileges, and the feeling that they belonged to something important. Several families related by blood lived together in households, with as many as fifty people sharing one house. Households were bound together into larger groups called clans. Clan members believed they were related through a common ancestor who lived long before.

Every household and clan had stories that told of how an ancestor had met some spirit, often in animal form, which had granted him or her privileges. This might be the knowledge of how to hunt certain animals, such as bears or whales. Or it might be the right to hunt in a specific place, wear a special mask, or use the animal as a totem. A Tlingit story tells of ancestors visiting the undersea home of Killer Whale where he gave the Tlingits the right to use the killer whale as a sign of the clan. Indians thought of these rights as property, like houses and canoes, to be passed on from generation to generation as valuable possessions.

The families who inherited the most important rights and privileges were the most important families of the tribes. Their leaders formed the upper or noble class.

The highest-ranking member of the most powerful family was the chief. Sometimes this was a woman, but most often the chief was a man. The chief was in charge of a council of nobles that gave advice. The chief had the power to make war and to decide when his or her people should move to temporary hunting and fishing places. Other responsibilities of the chief included giving permission to trade and deciding to have a totem pole carved.

Family members who did not have many inherited rights were commoners. They were considered less important than nobles. Most people were commoners.

LEFT: A TLINGIT BEAR CHIEF'S CLAN HAT.

BELOW: AN INDIAN WOMAN BEING BROUGHT TO THE VILLAGE OF HER INTENDED HUSBAND. MARRIAGES WERE USUALLY ARRANGED BY FAMILIES, WHO EXCHANGED GIFTS.

THIS WEAPON COULD
BE USED IN COMBAT
AS WELL AS FOR THE
EXECUTION OF A SLAVE.

The lowest members of the household were the slaves. They were men and women captured in war or purchased from nearby groups. Slaves were valuable property. Usually, they were well treated and were allowed to marry other slaves and have families. Sometimes, however, owners treated slaves less kindly. These slaves were sold, given away, or killed. In the households of chiefs and wealthy nobles, as many as half the people might be slaves.

The village was the center of life on the Northwest coast. The population was usually small, from fifty to several hundred people. Indians lived in permanent winter villages from about September to May. Then they moved to temporary camps near good hunting and fishing.

Favorite locations for permanent villages were at river mouths or in bays that gave the Indians protection from winter storms. The Indians built villages on sloping land overlooking beaches where canoes could be pulled up above the tide line.

Houses were usually built about twenty feet (6 m) apart facing the water in a single row. Larger villages had more rows of houses.

In a typical Big-House, people had to bend over to get through the low entrance. The inside was dark except for the light of cooking fires and some sunlight that came shining through the cracks between the side and roof boards. A large cooking area covered over a fourth of the floor space. Usually it was dug into the earth a foot (30 cm) or more. In the cooking area, each family living in the Big House had its own fire-pit. Roof boards were pushed open overhead to allow the smoke to escape. It still smelled smoky inside though.

Outside the cooking area was a floor of cedar boards. Higher up were several platforms that looked like big steps. The lower platforms held wooden storage boxes painted with totem designs. On the top platform, next to the outside wall, each family had a sleeping area. Mats or screens separated one family's space from another, which gave some privacy. The sleeping areas were covered with mats of cedar bark and furs. The house had little furniture except for storage boxes, baskets, and some backrests.

A TYPICAL NORTHWEST COAST INDIAN VILLAGE

TOP: THE INTERIOR OF A NOOTKA SOUND HOUSE.
NOTICE THE ELABORATELY CARVED SUPPORTING POSTS
AND CEILING RACKS USED FOR DRYING SALMON.
BOTTOM: HOUSES OFTEN HAD WOODEN PARTITIONS
SEPARATING ONE FAMILY'S SPACE FROM ANOTHER'S.

The largest living area was at the back of the Big-House. This belonged to the chief or leader of the household. Behind this space in some Big-Houses, a wall of boards painted with large totem designs made a storage area for household treasures. Most family members stayed out of this part of the house unless they were invited to enter.

Food was stored in the house, both in boxes near the sleeping areas and under the roof. Skin bags containing fish oil hung from the rafters. Also tied to the rafters over the fire were wooden poles on which fish and meat were dried and smoked for winter eating.

The totem pole people cooked the food from the ocean and forest at open fires both inside the Big-House and outside. They seldom used metal pots for cooking before trade with the white man developed. Nor did they use pottery in the way of most other Indians of North America. Women boiled food by putting red-hot stones into tightly woven baskets or boxes that were greased and filled with water. They cooked fish, shellfish, vegetable plants, and the meat from large animals in this way. Often they broiled fish and meat directly over the coals or wrapped them in leaves, such as those of the skunk cabbage, to be baked at the edge of the fire.

Northwest Indians ate large quantities of oil. They frequently dipped food in candlefish oil or animal fat during mealtimes. At special celebrations, so much valuable candlefish oil was eaten or burned that these occasions were known as "grease feasts."

Weather conditions influenced the clothing that people wore. In the warmth of summer days, men wore very little or went naked. Women wore only a short skirt or apron of woven bark. Sometimes men and women used moccasins. Usually they went barefoot.

During wet and colder weather, a variety of clothing provided protection and warmth. Coastal Indians used the skins or fur of deer, elk, bear, otter, mountain goat, seal, moose, and other animals for warm clothing. Some of the Tlingit wore buckskin shirts and trousers with feet sewn on them. Rainwear such as cloaks or capes made of woven cedar bark and basket-like hats kept the villagers dry.

The totem pole people loved decoration. They often made woven or painted designs on their clothing. Other decoration was added with fringes, porcupine quills, animal teeth, shells, hawk and eagle claws, and the beaks of birds called puffins.

Body decoration was also popular. Many people of the coast painted their faces or tattooed their bodies. Both men and women wore ear decorations of copper and beads and bracelets of copper, wood, bone, fur, and iron. Sometimes they inserted wood and bone

ABOVE: MUCH OF
THE CLOTHING
WORN BY COASTAL
INDIANS WAS MADE
OF ANIMAL SKINS
OR FUR. THIS CAPE,
HOWEVER, USED TO
KEEP DRY IN RAINY
WEATHER, WAS MADE
OF CEDAR BARK.

RIGHT: THIS TUNIC
OF MOUNTAIN GOAT
WOOL IS RICHLY
DECORATED.

plugs up to three inches (8 cm) wide through the nose or lips. The people of the greatest importance or wealth wore the most jewelry of this kind.

Some southern groups practiced head flattening among the members of their upper classes. They used cord and pads of cedar bark and wood to shape the soft foreheads of infants as they rested on their cradleboards. Over time, the front of the head became flattened and remained that way for life. Adults considered this a mark of great beauty and importance.

The life of children on the Northwest coast was probably easier and more carefree than in many other North American tribes. The land was rich, and children, like their parents, did not have to work hard all the time to survive. Until they were considered to be young adults, around their early teens, children helped their parents with the chores of daily life but spent much time in play.

Children played with toys that were considered correct for their sex. Boys had toy canoes and small versions of the bows and arrows their fathers and uncles used. Girls played with wooden dolls with hair made of bark or fur. Both boys and girls played a variety of games. Many were similar to the games children play today: tag, hide-and-seek, guessing games, and ball games.

In a tag game called fish trap, one child was the fish and the others were the fishermen. They joined hands and tried to catch the fish. Nootka children played a game much like king-of-the-hill. They formed two teams. A member of the first team buried a clam shell at the top of a sandpile, and then sat on the top as a guard. Teammates gathered around to protect him. The second team then attacked the hill and tried to uncover the shell.

Laughing games were popular with children and adults. Both individuals and teams played. People stared at their opponents with a serious, unhappy expression. Whoever smiled or laughed first was the loser. Children and adults also liked guessing games and various games of skill. Adults loved to gamble on the outcome of such activities.

Special events changed the regular day-to-day life of the village. During the winter ceremonials, the myths of family and clan came alive as the villagers acted out the old stories in song and dance. The actors wore beautiful costumes and wonderfully carved masks of many colors, shapes, and sizes. Another kind of special event was the potlatch.

The potlatch was a celebration of a great event in the life of a leader, his family, and the village. Most potlatches were small and marked personal events in the family such as a marriage, the building of a new

PARTICIPANTS IN A POTLATCH
OF THE 1800s

house, or the passing of children into adulthood. Other potlatches were large and expensive affairs given by a powerful leader to celebrate the raising of a new totem pole or to mark the life of an old chief who had recently died.

The word *potlatch* means "to give away" or "a gift giving." All guests invited to the potlatch received gifts. The bigger the potlatch, the more expensive were the gifts. Common presents were food, baskets, clothing, blankets, and jewelry. Gifts at big potlatches might include very valuable items such as slaves, canoes, and expensive copper tablets called "coppers." Those who received presents were expected to give away even greater presents at their own potlatches. In this way, wealth was passed around among the people. Sometimes, however, these valuables were not given away but were destroyed in front of the guests. This showed that they meant nothing to the owner. The more that was given away or destroyed at a potlatch, the more important the giver and his family were considered to be.

The largest potlatches were major events in the life of the village. These events might take several years to plan and prepare. Hundreds of guests were invited for days of feasting, music, dancing, drinking, gift-giving, and storytelling.

DRESSED FOR A POTLATCH, TLINGIT RESIDENTS STAND IN
FRONT OF AN ORNATELY CARVED SCREEN BEHIND WHICH
THE HOUSE CHIEF LIVED. MANY OF THE ITEMS ON THE
PLATFORMS ARE SERVING VESSELS USED WITH THE FEASTING
THAT ACCOMPANIED EVERY POTLATCH. BECAUSE A POTLATCH
COULD LAST AS LONG AS TWELVE DAYS, THE AMOUNT OF

FOOD OFFERED AND CONSUMED WAS TRULY TREMENDOUS.
SOMETIMES AT A POTLATCH THE CHIEF CALLED IN HIS RIVALS
AND, RIGHT IN FRONT OF EVERYONE, DESTROYED HIS ENTIRE
LIFETIME'S ACCUMULATION OF WEALTH. THE CARVED FIGURE
(LEFT) SYMBOLIZES THIS DESTRUCTION; IT IS AVERTING ITS
FACE AND SHIELDING IT FROM THE DEVOURING FLAMES.

The wealth achieved by the Indians of the totem pole lands made the expensive potlatches possible. In those parts of North America with less natural wealth, such events could not take place. It was one of the customs of the totem pole makers that white people found difficult to understand and accept when they came to the Pacific Northwest.

LIVING WITH THE WHITE MAN

The earliest known visit of a white man to the land of the totem pole makers was in the year 1592. Captain Juan de Fuca, a Greek explorer sailing for the Spanish government, planted the flag of Spain at Port Angeles, Washington.

The most famous of the early visitor-explorers was Captain James Cook of the British Royal Navy. He and his crew surveyed the Pacific Northwest coast from 1777 to 1779. Captain Cook kept a careful record of his explorations. His journals are an important early source of information about the totem pole Indians.

By the end of the 1700s, four nations had a strong interest in the Pacific Northwest: Spain, Great Britain, Russia, and the United States of America. Many Europeans and Americans wanted to trade for furs. In exchange for the skins of the sea otter, beaver, and other animals, the Indians received metal tools, weapons, blankets, and a variety of other manufactured goods. The fur trade reached its height from about 1780 to 1800. After that time, people in Canada and the United States become more interested in Indian lands than in furs.

Contact between whites and Indians sometimes resulted in war on the Northwest coast. Generally, though, things were peaceful. The Indians were small in number and, sandwiched between ocean and mountains, they had nowhere to escape.

The Indian way of life has changed greatly as a result of its contact with the white culture. The old ways have mostly disappeared. Many Indians were killed off by the white man's diseases, such as smallpox and measles, for which they had no resistance. As other Indians were attracted to the white culture and the things money could buy, there was less interest in preserving the old traditions. The knowledge needed to make skillful wood carvings, for example, almost died out completely. Sometimes the government disapproved of an Indian custom and forced people to change their ways. In the early 1900s, potlatches were banned as being wasteful and destructive. It was not until 1951 that this law was changed.

Over time, the American and Canadian governments have taken responsibility for the lands of the totem pole Indians. These lands were either directly taken over or set aside as reservations where Indians could live their own lives with government help. This was done through agreements called treaties. Sometimes the powerful white governments honored the treaties; sometimes they did not.

Today the people of the totem lands are still dealing with change. It is not easy for them. Many Indians of the Northwest have been able to make a successful living from trapping, hunting, fishing, guiding, crafts, farming, and ranching. Many others face serious problems such as unemployment, alcoholism, poor health, and poverty. It is a hopeful sign that the Indians in the land of the totem pole are working to preserve the best of their old way of life and to blend that with what is good in the new.

FOR FURTHER READING

Bancroft-Hunt, Norman. *People of the Totem: The Indians of the Pacific Northwest*. London: Orbis Publishing Ltd., 1979.

Burland, Cottie. Revised, Marion Wood. *North American Indian Mythology*. New York: Peter Bedrick Books, 1985 (original copyright 1965).

Erdoes, Richard, and Alfonso Ortiz, eds. *American Indian Myths and Legends*. New York: Pantheon Books, 1984.

Harris, Christie. *Once More Upon a Totem*. Toronto: McClelland and Stewart Ltd., 1973.

Holder, Glenn. *Talking Totem Poles*. New York: Dodd, Mead & Company, 1973.

INDEX

Map by Joe LeMonnier

[64]